Hi Five

By
NIECY JONES

ISBN: 0692823700
ISBN-13: 978-0692823705

iamEPE
www.iamEPE.com

DEDICATION

To all of the future Engineers of the World.

CONTENTS

ACKNOWLEDGMENTS

I would like to express gratitude to my parents, two former Educators, who instilled in me the belief that learning was fun. Also, many thanks to my third grade teacher, Mr. Emanuel, who planted the Author seed in my life. Lastly, to my Publisher, I AM EPE…We did it! Thank you for believing.

Hi, my name is One!

I like to have fun.

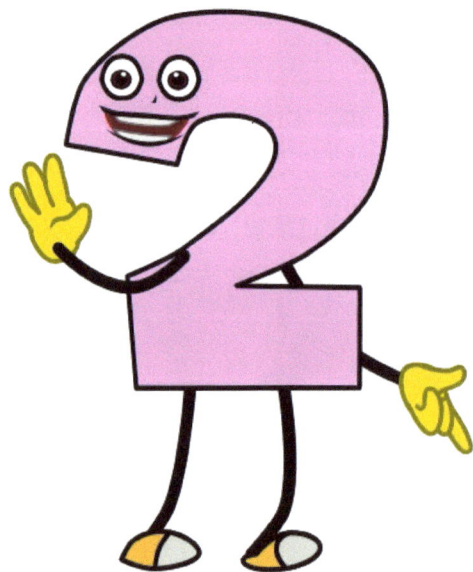

Hi, my name is Two!

I like my brand new shoes.

Hi, my name is Three!

I like to climb trees.

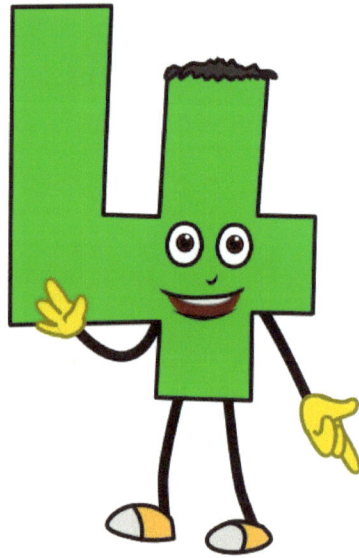

Hi, my name is Four!

I like it when I snore.

Hi, my name is Five!

I like to bike ride.

What is your name? What do you like?

Would you like to ride Five's bike?

Would **you** like to close the door, get in bed and snore like Four?

Would you like to laugh with glee, while you climb a tree like Three?

Would you like to wear Two's shoes, while you do all that you do?

Would you like to have some fun?

Can you count your new friends from one?

One!

Two!

Three!

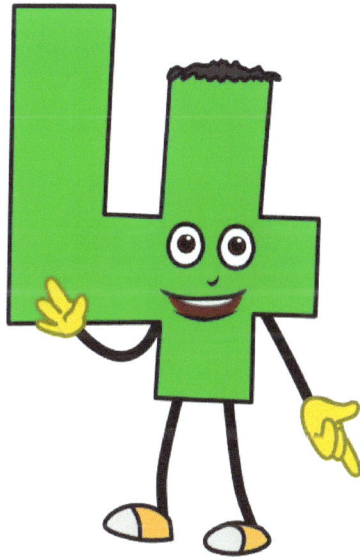

Four!

Five!

Now you know your new five friends.

Let's say bye, 'Till we meet again…

Bye!

ABOUT THE AUTHOR

Niecy Jones is an Electrical Engineer by day and avid learner by night. Born to a family of Educators, Niecy's passion for learning took hold at an early age. Her ideal that learning is fun exudes the pages of her writings.